Bayerische Verwaltung
der staatlichen Schlösser,
Gärten und Seen
Bavarian Administration of State
Castles, Palaces, Gardens, and Lakes

Peter O. Krückmann

The Land of Ludwig II

The Royal Castles and Residences
in Upper Bavaria and Swabia

Prestel
Munich · Berlin · London · New York

CONTENTS

Between Lake Constance to the the west and the Salzburg area to the east is a region which, in terms of its history and cultural treasures, can be matched by few regions in the world. Over the course of many centuries and during several different periods, a cultural landscape developed which today has since become the quintessence of the Bavarian identity.

The cultural origins of this area can be traced back to pre-Roman times and include one of the most ancient cities in Germany: Cambodunum, now known as Kempten. The settlement, founded shortly after the birth of Christ by Emperor Tiberius, is situated high above the River Iller on territory once occupied by the Celts. During the Middle Ages there was a flourish in cultural development which had far-reaching consquences following the founding of a number of large monasteries in this area. Benediktbeuern (739–40) is the oldest monastery in the lower alpine region of Bavaria. The establishment of monasteries at Tegernsee (before 746), Füssen (748), Polling (750), and Ottobeuren (764), as well as Frauenchiemsee and Herrenchiemsee (766), to mention just the most famous, followed in close succession. The founders were largely Bavarian and Frankish princes who, through these endowments, not only secured their own salvation and that of their subjects but also provided the decisive impetus to cultivate the countryside. Large tracts of forest were cleared and the terrain transformed into land suitable for agricultural purposes. All of the monasteries were also significant centers of art and science.

The 18th century witnessed a further cultural peak when propitious political circumstances, considerable wealth, and renewed faith among the population brought forth the Bavarian Rococo. The most famous Rococo building of this region, the **Wies Church**, the goal of many a pilgrim, was built here in 1743. Up until the end of the 18th century, this rugged, mountainous area instilled fear and awe in those who traveled through it, and an appreciation of nature and a delight in the majesty of the impressive Alps only started to gain general popularity towards the end of the 19th century. This was also true for King Ludwig II of Bavaria, even though the mountains were later to become his favorite retreat.

Here in this mountainous region, Ludwig's architectural visions became reality. In the period of some two decades from 1868, he commissioned the construction of **Neuschwanstein**, **Linderhof**, and **Herrenchiemsee**, as well as other properties such as at **Schachen**. Created as havens of solitude, today they attract millions of tourists every year, many of whom would consider a trip to Germany incomplete if they did not visit at least one of King Ludwig's "fairy-tale" castles.

Of the approximately eight hundred fortresses and castles which are to be found in Bavaria today, almost 50 of them are maintained by the Administration of Castles, Parks and Lakes in Bavaria. This makes the organization one of the most important owners of historical buildings in Germany. Its monuments are restored, maintained, and made accessible to today's visitors at great expense. The buildings, parks, and gardens of the lower alpine region, "the Land of King Ludwig II," are introduced in this illustrated volume. As one of four volumes it provides an introduction into the fascinating world of the fortresses and castles, parks and lakes of the former kingdom of Bavaria.

When the Wies Church—Bavaria's most famous pilgrimage church—was built during the Rococo period, Swabia was already a center of art and culture.

top: This portrait of King Ludwig II in an officer's uniform was painted by Wilhelm Tauber in 1864, shortly after Ludwig's accession to the throne (Ludwig II Museum at Herrenchiemsee).

Since his childhood, when he spent the summer months with his parents at Hohenschwangau, Ludwig had been familiar with the lower alpine region of Bavaria where he later had Neuschwanstein built.

THE RESIDENCE IN KEMPTEN

No other monastic complex so fully exemplifies the essence of the southern German foundations as does the residence of the prince-abbot of Kempten, who was both the spiritual head of the monastery as well as the worldly ruler of a vast territory once known as the "princely endowment of Kempten." In the manner of all Baroque princes, he required a magnificent setting as Ruler of the State in which life at court would reflect his high rank. In its expansive form, the residence of the prince-abbot perfectly exemplifies the German petty states' assertion of their power during the 17th and 18th centuries and, as far as its age is concened, it can be counted among the oldest monastic foundations from the Carolingian period. Its origins can be traced back as far as the year 730. At that time the monk Audogar of Sankt Gallen founded a mission cell on the banks of the Iller opposite the former Roman settlement Cambodunum. Only twenty-two years passed before the monastery in Kempten was founded, based on these modest beginnings. The acknowledged founder was the second wife of Charlemagne, Hildegard of Swabia, who was later canonized. The monastery fell under the onslaught of the Hungarians in 926, leading to its relocation on a knoll which at that time was still outside the town boundary. Following infeudation in 1213 with the county of Kempten, the abbots became sovereign princes of the Holy Roman Empire. As of 1361 Kempten was entitled to call itself a free city of the realm, poisoning the relationship between the endowment and the townspeople, and even provoking unbridled outbreaks of violence over a long period of time. The spread of the Reformation to the city in 1527 led to a further escalation of the conflict, which finally exploded in 1632 when the Swedes together with the Protestant free city reduced the monastery to "a mere heap of stones." Revenge was not long in coming, for directly afterward, imperial troops destroyed entire sections of the old city and massacred a third of the population. The reconstruction of the monastery complex as it stands today was begun in 1652 after the end of the Thirty Years War.

From an art historical point of view, the residence in Kempten is of great importance as the first monumental monastic complex of the Baroque in Germany. Accustomed to large buildings as we are today, it is perhaps difficult to immediately recognize the architectural significance of this structure from its outward appearance. This significance does not lie in the beauty of its formal details but rather in the power and self-assurance expressed by the massiveness of the construction which has virtually no subdivisions into smaller units.

The former Benedictine monastery with the collegiate church dedicated to St. Lorenz is the first monumental monastery complex completed after the Thirty Years' War. It became the model for numerous monasteries that were built later.

right: A detail of the wall in the prince-abbot's bedroom shows the high artistic quality of the delicate ornamentation. (Main picture)

The prince-abbot's rooms were decorated after 1735 by stucco-workers from Wessobrunn following the Rich Chambers of the electoral residence in Munich.

left: Through the harmonious interplay of stucco work, sculpture and painting, the Great Hall is not only the climax of the succession of princely apartments, but a prime example of a Rococo *gesamtkunstwerk*.

right: The allegorical sculpture of pacifism was created by the artist Aegid Verhelst from Antwerp, who assumed a leading role in Bavarian art of the 18th century.

Johann Georg Üblher was one of the most productive stucco-craftsmen of the Bavarian Rococo. He also created the stucco work in the throne room, including the relief with the allegory of architecture.

The paintings by Franz Georg Hermann in the study represent the princely virtues. The theme is picked up again in the ceiling painting, which shows the path of the Christian soul, guided into heaven with the help of the divine virtues.

Together with the monastery cathedral, standing imposingly on its hill, and built around two large square courtyards, the Vorarlberg architect Michael Beer (1605–1666) devised a complex which would serve as a model for many similar architectural undertakings during the century to follow.

When the prince-abbot Baron Anselm I of Meldegg had the state rooms remodeled in the 18th century in the style of the early Rococo, he created a unique ensemble. These rooms represent another outstanding artistic achievement with their filigree stucco work, decorative murals, doorcases framed in color and their ornamental parquet floors. On entering, one has to be reminded that this is actually a monastery. The series of rooms also demonstrates how a clerical prince's taste and need for representation closely resembled the artistic demands found in large cities throughout Europe.

The building was once entered through the central portal, although the location of the entrance has since been moved. After passing through an antechamber, the visitor reaches the splendid, two-story Great Hall, the center of the state apartments and the entire monastic residence, by ascending a flight of steps. It is only fitting that it has been referred to as "one of the most exquisite rooms of the Bavarian-Swabian Rococo." Polished stucco marble, mirrors, and sparkling chandeliers, as well as a vast ceiling painting unequivocally demonstrate the prince's magnitude and importance to the dazzled visitor. Franz Georg Hermann's fresco is dedicated to the glory of the princely foundation and the history of its inception. Together with the exceptionally fine figurative sculptures by Aegid Verhelst representing the princely virtues of pacifism, love, strength, and wisdom, the throne room clearly manifests the political-historical legitimation of this ecclesiastical principality.

Jacob's Dream of the Ladder to Heaven, the ceiling painting by Franz Georg Hermann in the prince-abbot's bedroom is an encoded depiction of his own ascension to heaven.

Passing through the library, the audience chamber is reached. Here Hermann created the highly allusive ceiling painting *The Queen of Sheba before King Solomon's Throne.* The clearly conveyed message is of the prince-abbott of Meldegg comparing himself to the wisest of all kings, the righteous Solomon,

to whom even a ruler as wealthy and powerful as the Queen of Sheba is paying homage! Referring to Kempten, this is an identification which today might make us smirk; in the 18th century, however, the age of late absolutism, such pompous displays of one's own self-worth were nothing out of the ordinary.

The series of rooms leads into the study with its impressive marquetry cabinets, and then to the bedroom. Since the time of the Sun King Louis XIV, rising in the morning and going to bed at night were highlights of court ceremony. The furnishings of this room are correspondingly opulent and pick up on the theme of the ceiling painting with its allegorical depiction of the evening sky. In the rear half of the room, where the abbot's magnificent bed stood, the painting *Jacob's Dream of the Ladder to Heaven* which he commissioned can be seen. It would appear that such an image in a bedroom was nothing unusual. Yet another, more far-reaching theme is depicted alongside that of sleep. In the same way that Jacob dreamed that a ladder on which angels moved up and down was extended to him from heaven, this image became a symbol of a mortal's spiritual path to heaven and his reception there—for the abbot, it represents a hidden apotheosis of himself! Self-allegories like this can commonly be found in worldly contexts, and it was not considered blasphemous if a ruler commissioned images illustrating his own entry into heaven. In ecclesiastical buildings, a representation of this type would have been condemned as conceit of the highest order.

The succession of princely apartments ends with the court chancellery, an unpretentious corner room with a bay window. Decisive events such as the Reformation or the Thirty Years War were considered brief or occasional dangers to the monastery. It was finally secularization which led to the demise of the centuries-old tradition of the prince-abbots. The splendid rooms also became superfluous, and no one knew quite what to do with them. Ultimately, they were used as offices and only following extensive renovation work in 1992 have they once again been returned their former glory and made accessible to the public.

In the bedroom, sculptured putti hold up a painting depicting the Madonna of Sorrows underneath a heavenly canopy.

opposite page, top: Ferdinand Piloty's painting of 1865 shows the young Ludwig in a general's uniform and coronation vestments. Today, both the robe and the painting are on display at Herrenchiemsee, the crown is in the treasure-vault of the royal residence in Munich.

opposite page, bottom left: Not far from Berg Castle, a cross in Lake Starnberg indicates the place where King Ludwig was found drowned together with his physician, von Gudden.

Ludwig had just turned eighteen when, in 1864, he was crowned "Bavaria's youngest and most handsome king" following the death of his father Maximilian II. He soon won the hearts of the great majority of his subjects with his charming and courteous personality, but at that point no one could foresee the extent to which Ludwig was unwilling to let himself be reduced to a mere "signature machine." He declared that that was his fate as a constitutional monarch and that his ideal was something quite different, namely the concept of absolute power as personified by Louis XIV. This ideal, which by that time had long since become an anachronism, was nurtured in him by historical fact and by German heroic legends familiar to him from the murals in his parents' castle Hohenschwangau. Tantalizing reports about the exotic Orient also gave wing to his all too receptive fantasy. Yet all this is not enough for us to form a clear understanding of the person known as "the fairy-tale king." He himself reported in a letter that his youth was anything but happy. He experienced his childhood as a "chain of humiliating torments" which certainly contributed to the sensitive Ludwig's retreating ever deeper into his fantasy world. The contemporary political situation also deeply embittered him. Until the founding of the German Reich in 1870, he was obliged to watch how Prussia pushed for hegemony in Germany, and that at the expense of the sovereignty of the constituent states. Seen in this context, Ludwig's immense building activity, which continued until his unexplained death in 1886, seems to be a sign of his stubborn self-assertion.

right: Among the king's legendary pastimes were sleigh-rides by night which started out from Linderhof. Painting by R. Wenig, c. 1885/86 (Marstallmuseum at Nymphenburg Palace).

NEUSCHWANSTEIN

Things just couldn't be done fast enough. In 1868, only four years after his coronation, the twenty-three year old king Ludwig II ordered the drafting of plans for a castle to be built within view of his parents' seat Hohenschwangau. From impressions engraved in his mind from his time at Hohenschwangau, Ludwig II followed the tradition of medieval chivalry. Starting with the original idea of a small building of almost playful lightness, a plan soon grew for a monumental castle in a neo-Romanesque style. In 1880 the basic structure of Neuschwanstein, which is at the same time a fortress and a royal residence, had been finished; the entire complex however was only completed in 1892, after the king's death. Only the principal rooms in the castle, the living quarters and state rooms, however, would be furnished during Ludwig II's lifetime.

A long drive winds up to the crenelated gateway flanked by corner towers. Behind it, first the lower, then, above that, the upper courts, are surprisingly spacious. A church was originally planned to be built in the latter. Surrounding the court, to the north and opposite the living quarters, is the knights' house, and towering above everything is the main building, comprising the royal apartments and the throne room. The route through the castle leads the visitor past some rooms which remain incomplete before leading to the impressive kitchen. The third floor above ground-level can be reached by a spiral staircase giving access to the throne room on one side and to the king's private living quarters on the other. The antechamber, a wedge-shaped area with groin vaults, forms a link between them. Illustrations from legends which decorate the walls here as well as in most of the other rooms, turn the castle into a walk-through picture book.

Originally Neuschwanstein was intended as a "temple" to Richard Wagner. *Tristan and Isolde, Lohengrin, Tannhäuser,* and *Die Meistersinger* were the operas from which the motifs for the murals were supposed to be taken. The lord of the castle, however, finally ordered that the decoration of the rooms should not be based on the operas themselves, but on the original sagas. In that way Ludwig hoped to avoid making the rooms seem to be mere illustrations of the operas composed by his father's

Picture-postcard scenery: Neuschwanstein with Lake Alp behind it; to the right Hohenschwangau Castle and, in the background, the silhouette of the Schlicken mountain.

inset: Neuschwanstein as seen from the south, showing the progress of construction by November 1881. Photo: Ludwig Schradler and Son, Füssen.

above: A few days after his accession to the throne in 1864 Ludwig invited Richard Wagner to Munich: the beginning of a momentous relationship. Detail from a painting by Fritz Bergen, c. 1890

previous double page:
The upper court is surrounded by the main building, the living quarters to the left and the knights' house on the opposite side.

top: Ludwig loved the distant views from Neuschwanstein, here seen from the balcony of the throne room to Lake Alp, with Hohenschwangau Castle to the right.

center: Landscape and technology in harmony: the filigree iron bridge across the Pöllat gorge to the south of the castle.

left: Elaborately woven and richly embroidered fabrics decorate the rooms; here the bay-window of the bedroom.

After his legal incapacitation, Ludwig was arrested in his bedroom on June 11, 1886, and taken to Berg castle.

friend. For the king something else mattered: namely with Neuschwanstein he envisioned resurrecting Mont Salvat, the mythical castle of the Holy Grail. For him the world of the Grail was the most chivalrous and exalted form of Christian endeavor. Recent art historical research has only now been able to clarify how such notions can be explained solely on the basis of Ludwig's own life history. The gravely oppressive conflict he endured between a guilt-ridden eroticism, with which he struggled throughout his life, and his resultant deep longing for purity and holiness, weighed heavily on him. Sin and salvation are the basic concepts based on which the legends to be illustrated were chosen.

From the forecourt, the king's apartments were originally approached from the adjunt's room and the workroom following on from it. Today's tour only allows one to see the apartments "backwards," beginning with the intimate rooms first. Passing through an anteroom, the king's dining room is reached. Here the visitor is introduced to the world of minnesingers at the court of

Ludwig, who was a very religious man, had a private chapel built adjacent to his bedroom, consecrated to a king who shares his name, Saint Louis IX of France.

Count Hermann of Thuringia. Over the doors are the portraits of famous singers: Gottfried von Strassburg, Wolfram von Eschenbach, and Reinmar von Zweter. The actual theme of the minnesingers' poems is alluded to here: the pure—as opposed to the physical—love of a woman. Their ulterior meaning is that of the Virgin Mary transposed into the worldly realm. The love poems sung by the minnesingers also stand for the conquest over all that is "evil and base" in mankind, represented here by the elaborate bronze sculpture *Siegfried Slaying the Dragon* on the dining room table. In all this, Ludwig created a monument to himself.

In the next room, the bedroom, and in the small chapel adjacent, there is a change of styles to the Gothic. This interplay with artistic styles is not an

expression of the master's whim. The king was quite consciously trying to make a meaningful statement. The Romanesque period, which otherwise characterizes the entire castle, was supposed to allude to the ancient origins of the legends. The Gothic style, on the other hand, familiar from cathedral architecture, adds an aura of holiness. For Ludwig, the bedroom was by no means a place of intimate pleasure, but should rather be understood as a type of monk's cell—albeit one splendid enough for a king. The denial of sensual-ity is also the theme of the paintings: Tristan takes leave of Isolde and thus also of earthly love. They are re-united only in death—and Ludwig could contemplate this paragon of salvation in holiness from his reading chair. The altar painting in the house chapel, bathed in the mystical light of the stained glass window, depicts a saint who shares the king's name—Saint Louis IX of France.

After passing through two more rooms, the visitor reaches the spacious living room, divided by an arched opening. The theme in the murals is the Lohengrin legend. The picture sequence culminates in the Gobelin showing the election of Lohengrin by the Holy Grail, the so-called miracle of the Grail. When Ludwig sat on the bench beneath it, with a table next to him covered by an embroidered cloth bearing the image of a swan—the leitmotif of Neuschwanstein—he must have felt drawn into the world of Lohengrin, the swan knight.

The passageway leading off the living room comes as a surprise, for here—on the third floor above ground-level—the king had a small grotto

Just as in the bedroom, the dressing room also has a bay-window. Here, Ludwig kept a casket in which he kept his jewellery.

Ludwig enjoyed reading or dreaming in the 'Schwaneneck' (Swan's Corner), an alcove adjacent to the living room.

constructed, an allusion to the Venus grotto which appears again in painted form in the last of the king's rooms, the study. The cycle of murals shows scenes from the Tannhäuser legend: in a certain sense a recapitulation of themes expressed throughout the entire decorative scheme. The minstrel Tannhäuser succumbed to temptation and entered the Venusberg where he abandoned himself to the sensuality of its mistress. On another large mural opposite this image, he sings to the glory of the goddess of love, much to the dismay of the knights who are gathered there. Like Tristan, it is only in death that Tannhäuser finds his pure, chaste love for the countess, Elisabeth, who was later to be canonized. King Ludwig saw in this a mirror of the drama in his own life.

In a certain sense the apotheosis—the transfiguration of the king who longed for salvation—takes place in the mighty throne room on the opposite side of the castle. After following the guided route through the relatively homely, wood-paneled rooms of the rather dimly lit living apartments, one is stunned by the cool, gold-shimmering opulence and bright light of these unexpectedly spacious rooms. Suddenly it is as though one has entered a Byzantine church. This structure was modelled on the Hagia Sophia in Istanbul as well as on the historicist palace church of All Saints in the royal residence in Munich.

In the raised apse of this church-like throne room, it was planned that steps of white Carrara marble would lead to an ivory throne (also in the symbolic color of purity) decorated with gold under a free-standing baldachin. But this

room was never to be completed. It was surely not Ludwig's intention to hold court here, nor is it clear whether Ludwig meant to position his throne in the place of an altar for himself as the King of Bavaria. In the Castle of the Grail legend, much more interest is focussed on "the unknown king of the Grail" for whose arrival the room was constructed. Today it is an accepted fact that Ludwig secretly identified with him in his fantasy world. This is not only suggested

There are numerous depictions showing Ludwig as the swan knight Lohengrin. Lithography by Hans Stubenrauch, Munich.

The landscape artist A. Dirigel constructed a grotto for Ludwig (on the third floor above ground-level) so that he could reenact the saga of Lohengrin, who rested in the Venus grotto, as realistically as possible.

20

by the painted row of six canonized kings who are shown standing between stylized palms—symbols of eternal life—with Louis of France in the center. This assumption is also supported by the image of Saint George slaying the dragon on the rear wall of the throne room. The decoration on Saint George's helmet identifies him as the swan knight and lord of Neuschwanstein, which can be seen on a cliff in the background. For the most part, the remaining murals illustrate the exploits of the princely saints and the triumph of Christianity.

A dragon guards the entrance to the singers' hall at the top of the spiral staircase which was reserved for the king only.

Returning to the antechamber and climbing the spiral staircase, the visitor reaches the fourth story where the impressive singers' hall is located above the king's living quarters. The newel post at the end of the staircase has the form of a palm tree reaching up into a starry sky. Ludwig, who consciously planned every element with a view to its symbolism, found a pictorial means to transform this act of climbing into a symbol of the striving for transcendence from an imperfect life on earth into an eternal, divine realm.

Second only to the throne room, the singers' hall is the most important room in the castle. Ludwig found inspiration for its design in a similar room at Wartburg, in Thuringia. As in that medieval castle, the room here is open to a raised passageway along one length. The room's location under the roof as well as the podium at one end are clearly borrowed from the older castle. This resemblance is certainly not the result of mere imitation. More importantly, Ludwig had his castle designed in an apparent effort

left: The throne room, shaped like a Byzantine church, seems to be decorated with the most precious stones and mosaics. In fact, the columns are made of coloured stucco and the depictions are merely painted.

above: The crown-shaped chandelier is based on examples from the Middle Ages such as the one in Aachen Cathedral, intendend to symbolise the Heavenly Jerusalem.

23

to achieve historical authenticity, for the famous war of the singers, also the subject of Wagner's *Tannhäuser*—an opera which had deeply moved the young crown prince—is said to have taken place in the early 13th century in the same room at the Wartburg. And the *Minnesang*, the glorification of "pure love," is certainly a central, iconographical theme throughout the castle. The pictorial representation, however, only takes the art of singing into consideration to a very small degree. The Parsifal legend is of central importance here, and in this regard, the room at Neuschwanstein completely departs from its prototype, which is decorated with images of heroes and saints. Ludwig also elevated this room beyond its function as a room for festivities to that of a room for worship, fully in keeping with the total concept behind Neuschwanstein.

Seen from an art historical point of view, Neuschwanstein is recognized as one of the most important examples of Historicism. But for tourists traveling to it from all over the world, this castle perched imposingly on a steep rock outcrop seems quintessentially medieval. It might be rewarding to pause and think about how it came to be, and why Neuschwan-stein just seems like a figment of our imagination or a magic spell summoning a long-gone epoch. Neuschwanstein is the dream-become-reality of the strong-willed "fairy-tale king" who refused to accept any external limitations which threatened the image of himself as a ruler. Nowadays, however, the visitor has the fascinating possibility of glimpsing into Ludwig's chambers which were strictly off-limits to strangers during the monarch's lifetime and of contemplating the impressive, picturesque appeance of the castle. Neuschwanstein, set before a majestic backdrop of mountains, is indeed a virtuoso theatrical production and a combination of art and nature.

right: The singers' hall underneath the roof of the main building was inspired by a Munich performance of Wagner's opera *Tannhäuser*. The original model was the historic singers' hall in Wartburg Castle.

left: The kitchen houses the latest technology of the time. The grill in the background is operated automatically by a turbine which is powered by the hot air of the fire, while the steam of the stove is drawn off downwards and used to warm the table-ware in the wall cupboards.

Neuschwanstein at night: King Ludwig would have enjoyed such lighting effects.

LINDERHOF

Leaving the plain around Füssen the journey through the "Land of Ludwig II" leads into the remote Graswang valley. Ever since he was a young prince, Ludwig had been familiar with this region as his father had built a small hunting lodge there. He felt drawn to the remote mountain valley because of its proximity to the Ettal monastery, founded by King Ludwig the Bavarian in 1330, which he thought of as a type of Castle of the Holy Grail. The architecture of the monastery church and its striking dome, which today still possesses most of

its original Gothic elements, seemed to allude to that. Following his visit to Versailles in 1867, the king dreamed of building his own palace here. He called the project "Meicost Ettal," an anagram derived from the alleged declaration of Louis XIV, "L'état, c'est moi." At the same time, the name could be made to sound like the English words "my castle." Quite simply, however, the name was nothing less than a statement of his intentions.

Here in "his" castle, withdrawn from the eyes of the world and far from reality, Ludwig wanted to live out his dream of the perfect kingdom which he believed Louis XIV had achieved. This could only happen in a fantasy world; the real world looked very different. Unrefined, without feeling, without understanding for unusual ideas: this was Ludwig's experience of his contemporaries after popular opinion had forced him to dismiss his father's friend Richard Wagner from Munich, and after his plan to give the city of Munich a Wagner festival hall had been turned down. Here, in the solitude of the mountains, the reclusive king could shelter from the lack of understanding and ill will.

In the meantime, the designs for "Meicost Ettal" became more and more elaborate until Ludwig finally decided to build his new Versailles on the island Herrenchiemsee. In the Graswang valley, a "royal villa," as Linderhof was first called, was created instead. Although a totally different type of building, several references to the original French prototype are unmistakable—not least in the numerous representations of the two Louis': Louis XIV and Louis XVI. It seems that Ludwig II felt particularly comfortable at Linderhof. During his time there he could abandon himself to his dream worlds of "1001 Nights," the Germanic sagas, the Middle Ages, and the Ancien Régime. In the spacious park he had the Moorish Kiosk and the Moroccan House erected, as well as the Venus Grotto,

Despite the difficulty of building in an alpine mountain valley above Oberammergau, Linderhof was erected in only six years, starting in 1868.

right: The castle is surrounded by an extensive park in the English style, which almost unnoticeably runs into the unspoiled countryside of the Graswang valley.

Although Linderhof was commissioned as a refuge for a king, its looks cannot obscure the fact that it was inspired by the upper middle class villas of the late 19th century.

the Hunding Cottage, and the Hermitage of Gurnemanz. Many more structures were also planned: an Arabian pavilion and a Baroque castle chapel, imitations of the Cuvilliés Theater and the Amalienburg in Munich, as well as a medieval fortress and a Chinese palace of enormous dimensions.

At first sight, Neuschwanstein and Linderhof seem to be worlds apart: the former an allusion to the mystical Middle Ages, the latter a revival of the luminous 18th century. Yet seen from Ludwig's ahistorical, subjective point of view, the differences become blurred. The fantasy of the still dreamily idealistic young king was filled with longing for a patriarchically-ruled society sheltered by harmony—a paradise on earth—as he saw it. Ludwig could realize his ideal by playing the role Lohengrin, the King of the Grail, or the sacrosanct king of French absolutism in his daydreams. It is significant that in the culture of both epochs, "love" which brings harmony—the central concept in Ludwig's mind—is a value of exceptional importance, manifested in the subtle forms of medieval German love poems and gallantry.

When standing in front of the miniature palace, the visitor has the impression of looking at villa, albeit an extraordinarily splendid one. The temple-like central structure, with its gable of figures framing the Bavarian coat of arms and holding up the royal crown, leaves no doubt as to the status of the resident. Like the god Atlas, whose figure towers over the heavens, the entire firmament weighs on his shoulders. Inside the building, the visitor is completely surrounded by the atmosphere of a Baroque castle. The equestrian statue of the Sun King in the vestibule unequivocally tells us to whom the house is dedicated. Ludwig's living quarters are on the upper floor, the *piano nobile*. Two magnificent staircases, inspired by the no longer extant "Ambassador's Steps" in Versailles, lead

above left: The western Gobelin room is also called the music chamber because of the 'aeludicum' that was set up there, an instrument combining elements of the harmonium and piano.

Although the audience room is
largely modelled on the one at
Versailles, the lavish decoration
mirrors the taste of the 19th
century.

The silverware container in the shape of a ship and decorated with the emblem of the Sun King was created by F. Brochier and E. Wollenweber the Younger, 1883/84.

to the upper floor. The decoration of rooms, symmetrically grouped around the stair hall, are all variations on a theme, namely Ludwig's identification with the age of the Bourbons. Large-format paintings on tapestry dominate both corner rooms along the main front. Themes from Ovid's *Metamorphoses* are shown in the room on the right, glorifying the love of the gods; idyllic landscapes and shepherd scenes decorate the room on the left. Since the Renaissance, visual narratives like these were familiar symbols of the Golden Age. Between the Gobelin rooms is the cleverly constructed Hall of Mirrors in which all registers of the neo-Baroque are pulled in delightful exaggeration.

 Highlights in the side wings of the castle are the audience room to the west and the dining room to the east, both constructed on an oval ground plan. Of course the reclusive king never received ambassadors here, which is why the audience room was put to private use as a study. This also explains the somewhat surprising placement of a particularly opulent writing table under the baldachin.

 The dining room, located on the other side of the building, is also a room for solitude and does not even have a large table. Ludwig's cupbearer reports in his memoirs that the king "tended to take his meals in the company of imaginary guests." Numerous similar observations have been preserved which all confirm that the lonesome king

In the dining room, a line around the table can be seen in the floor. Hidden underneath is the lift for raising or lowering the table.

30

The rose cabinet adjacent to the bedroom served the king as a dressing room. Set into the walls are portraits of prominent members of the Versailles court.

conjured up entire court parties in his mind. In order not to be disturbed in these reveries, he had the famous, mechanically-operated table installed in the middle of the room which was set by servants on the floor below, then raised through a trap door into the dining room. Referred to as "The Wishing Table," it is based on a motif in the well-known Grimms' fairy-tale *The Wishing Table, the Gold Ass, and the Cudgel-in-the-Sack.*

The bedroom too, in the northern wing of the castle, is also designed to be a haven of peace and solitude. It is an astonishingly large room for such a relatively small building, and also the most sumptuously furnished. It is just about every bit as magnificent as its prototype, the grand bedroom in the Residence in Munich, designed in 1730 by Cuvilliés. The only explanation for

31

the importance given to this room can be found in the analogy to the palace of Versailles where the Sun King's bedroom forms the center of the enormous complex.

Linderhof was designed to fit into the symmetric plan of a garden based on a Baroque prototype. A long waterfall cascades in a series of steps down the slope which rises behind the castle. It is no coincidence that a lily-shaped flowerbed filled with blue blossoms is placed just below the king's bedroom.

As in all of Ludwig's bedrooms, the one in Linderhof also features velvet fabrics in blue, the king's favourite color, with some embroidery in gold.

The music pavilion—from where the view extends right across the park to the silhouette of the Ammergau mountains—is reached along pathways winding up the hill and enclosed by flowering trellises.

The landscaped section of the twenty-acre park begins behind the rows of trees and hedges which surround the Baroque castle like a picture frame. It is dedicated to the fantasy of a king lost to the real world. Buildings scattered throughout the park, and at one time even beyond its borders, mark the stations of his dream journey through distant myths and exotic lands.

From the music pavilion, steps lead up to the legendary Venus Grotto. As natural as it appears, it is nonetheless an artificially created illusion—a three-dimensional stage set. This Hörsel Mountain, from the first act of Wagner's *Tannhäuser*, was recreated with iron supports and cement. Inside is the Venus Grotto, a thirty-foot-high dripstone cavern, together with two smaller grottos. An artificial lake occupies most of the space. From Ludwig's "royal seat," the shell throne—and even more fairy-tale-like—from a golden shell-shaped boat in which he was rowed over the lake, the king could soak up the magical atmosphere and watch dramas presented behind the stage-like opening come to life: Tannhäuser, who erred from the virtuous path of pure love to abandon himself to the charms of Venus and her playmates. Ludwig spared no expense in making the staging of this fantasy as dream-like as possible. Twenty-four generators were installed, creating Bavaria's first power station, so that rotating panes of glass in intense colors could produce downright psychedelic effects.

When he ordered the Moorish Kiosk to be resited at Linderhof, Ludwig employed widely diverse stylistic elements taken from Islamic art to realize his fantasies. He bought the kiosk in 1876, nine years after a Berlin architect designed it as the Prussian entry for the World Fair in Paris. The iron and wooden

Stretching in front of the castle is a French parterre, framed by arboured walks of trimmed lime and beech trees.

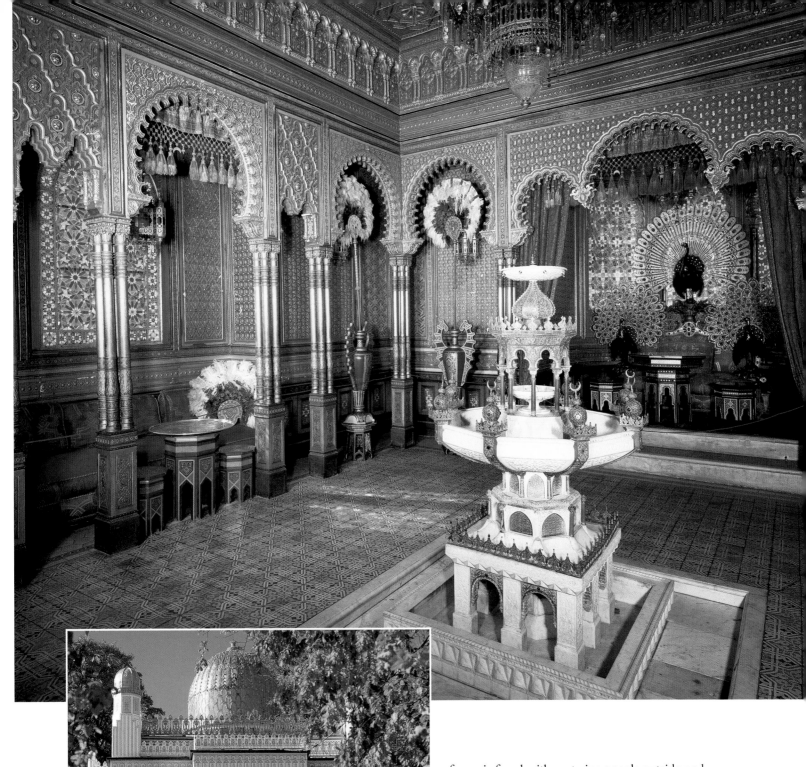

A perfect illusion of the Orient in the midst of the Bavarian Alps: the Moorish Kiosk (*above*). This little mosque-like structure is hidden in the forest that surrounds the grounds at Linderhof.

left: The artificial Venusberg grotto from the Tann-häuser legend was built in 1867–77. Ludwig was rowed over the little lake and it is said that he also enjoyed bathing here with changing illumination.

frame is faced with cast zinc panels outside and plaster inside. Despite the technical qualities of its construction, once inside, its atmosphere is dazz-ling. What little natural light there is falls into the building through stained glass windows and pro-duces a magical effect similar to that in the Venus Grotto. The focus of the modest-sized kiosk is the semi-circular apse in the rear wall, a later addition created according to the king's wishes. This is where the throne is positioned which itself is a fantastic recreation of the peacock throne of Persia. Once again, the throne served no official purpose. On the contrary: Ludwig could be alone here, and he let the room work its spell on him, dreaming of another world.

The Moorish Kiosk had hardly been completed when Ludwig commis-sioned another structure to be built, this time in the Islamic style. It was to be a

The façade of the Moroccan House is brightly painted with red and white stripes. Ludwig originally had it built in the remote mountain pasture known as the Stockalpe.

castle complex with a courtyard modelled on the Alhambra in Granada. Yet this project proved too costly even for King Ludwig, so instead he purchased the Moroccan House, a relatively spacious building, at the Paris World Fair of 1878. The king had it rebuilt in a mountain pasture called the Stockalpe, whereby numerous decorative elements were changed. Following Ludwig II's death the building was sold. It was finally reacquired by the Administration of Castles, Parks and Lakes in Bavaria in 1980 and restored. Leaving the park to the west, it can be seen slightly hidden in the forest above the main path.

At the extreme eastern end of the park is the cottage known as the Hundinghütte—a reconstruction of the original building which burned down in 1945. At one time it stood some distance from Linderhof at the foot of the 6,500-foot-high Kreuzspitze. Its appearance matches that of Hunding's apartment as described in Richard Wagner's *Valkyrie*. According to the story, the primitive forest cottage of roughly hewn wood was "built around the trunk of a mighty ash tree, whose branches grew right through the timber roof." The king commissioned the building of the Hundinghütte only a few days after seeing *The Ring of the Nibelung* at the first Bayreuth festival in 1876.

The Hundinghütte, a 'walk-in stage set' taken from Richard Wagner's *Valkyrie*, plunges the visitor into the world of Germanic myths and legends.

One year later, and this time inspired by Wagner's *Parsifal*, the king had the 'Einsiedelei des Gurnemanz' (Hermitage of Gurnemanz) erected—a structure that became dilapidated over the years but which has recently been reconstructed near the Hundinghütte. It is a cabin made of rough logs with a roof of bark. A bell turret in front of the gable end of the building lends it the character of a hermitage. Today the building can only be seen from the outside since the interior furnishings have been lost.

With these reconstructions of Wagnerian stage sets, Ludwig again made use of motifs he had already incorporated in the decoration of Neuschwanstein—partly in the form of murals, but partly also in a similarly realistic way. Once more these images are an expression of the king's profound longing for salvation—although the effect in such a bucolic setting is not at all as gloomy or oppressive.

opposite page, top: In the center of the water basin between the residence and the Venus Temple, a fountain powered by gravity from a sloping water conduit, shoots up a ninety-foot jet of water. Rising in front of the terrace is the lime tree, now more than 300-years-old, that gave the residence its name.

bottom: The Hermitage of Gurnemanz was built after Wagner's specifications in the libretto of his opera *Parsifal*. (From the historical archives).

A winding path leads through the park to the Temple of Venus and back into another world. After the enchanted, fairy-tale corners, the visitor is confronted with the symmetrical, neo-Baroque flower beds in front of the residence. From up on the terrace, the view stretches from the Monopteros across this historical landscaped park, with the three hundred-year-old lime tree to the left which lent Linderhof its name (Lime Estate or Manor), and to the large pool and its ninety-foot fountain. Beyond is the white residence and the cascade— a wonderful and carefully composed ensemble.

SCHACHEN

Stout shoes are recommended for a hike to the royal hunting lodge at Schachen, starting out from either Garmisch-Partenkirchen or Elmau. It takes several hours winding up into the mountains along a steep path which Ludwig had made into a bridleway in 1869. However, the effort is more than rewarding when Schachen, perched at an altitude of some 5,600 feet, is finally reached. The hunting lodge, and its servants' quarters, kitchen, and stables were built for the king out of wood in the so-called "Swiss Style" between 1870 and 1872. This proud structure is framed by the bare rock face of the Wetterstein range. The altitude reached only really becomes clear after walking a few more steps to the "Salettel"—a viewpoint from where there is a breathtaking vista deep into the Reintal, a glacial valley carved into the massif of Germany's highest mountain, the Zugspitze, or when looking down into the Loisach river valley with Partenkirchen in the distance. As is typical of all buildings commissioned by

Ludwig, this royal lodge is impressive if only for its spectacular location and the successful symbiosis with its overwhelmingly beautiful surroundings.

The wide ground floor seems somewhat squat, being overwhelmed by the size of the upper story, as if two structures had been built one on top of the other. The visitor senses that a special room is hidden behind the filigree wooden ornamentation of the balcony. Once inside, the strikingly cozy atmosphere of pine-panelled rooms is felt immediately. The parlor, the study, and Ludwig's bedroom, as well as the guest room and the footman's room seem simple but still royally substantial.

A narrow spiral staircase leads to the upper floor, as if the king wanted to shield himself from the outside world as much as possible to seek out a place of refuge. The surprising world in which the visitor is now engulfed provides the most extreme contrast imaginable to the rugged mountain slopes outside—as the room is decorated in a pure, oriental style. An engraving of a palace room in Constantinople was the prototype for the Turkish Hall at Schachen. The fairy-tale atmosphere was the king's special wish, and was carefully created by adding sumptuous furnishings such as carpets and embroidered textiles, a fountain, candelabras, and stands for peacock feathers. Together with the colored, refracted light coming from the red, yellow, and blue stained-glass window, these elements cast a unique spell on the room. With a hint of irony Luise von Kobell reported how the king spent his time there. She described how "Ludwig II sat

left: Light and dark in the mountains: the silhouette of the hunting lodge at Schachen reflected on the clouds above a mountain valley in the Wetterstein mountains.

The toils of the climb are redeemed: view beyond the royal hunting lodge to the Ester range near Garmisch-Partenkirchen.

At a height of close to 1,900 metres above sea level, this Swiss Style chalet is reached. It symbolises the lonely king's longing for seclusion.

in a Turkish costume reading while his group of servants, dressed as Muslims, lounged around on the carpets and cushions, smoking tobacco and sipping mokka according to the orders of their the royal master who often smiled slightly superciliously as his gaze wandered over the edge of his book to the group. All the while, trays of incense smoked and large peacock feather fans were swayed through the air in order to make the illusion more convincing."

Ludwig's fascination for the Orient was in many ways the expression of a widely popular trend at that time. Even in the 17th century, after chinoiserie had become the artistic style favored in court circles, the Far East had the reputation of being a paradise on earth. In the 19th century, these imaginings were also common among the urban middle classes, whereby the object of their fantasies extended to include the mystery of the *Felix Arabia*. King Ludwig's desire to create a retreat at Schachen was not so much fuelled by the mere dream of originality or his love of splendor, but much more by his search for inaccessible remoteness and his necessity to live out his dream of a different kind of world, a world of beauty and harmony, without being disturbed.

Ludwig must have loved his mountain retreat very much for he often spent some time here. Generally he stayed in Schachen around his birthday on August 25, and twice later on in the fall. Today, hikers who come here during the summer months also can visit the Alpine Garden directly in front of the hunting lodge, with its large display of alpine flowers created by the Munich Botanical Garden at the turn of the century.

The contrast between the exterior and the interior could not be any greater: the Turkish Hall at Schachen.

HERRENCHIEMSEE

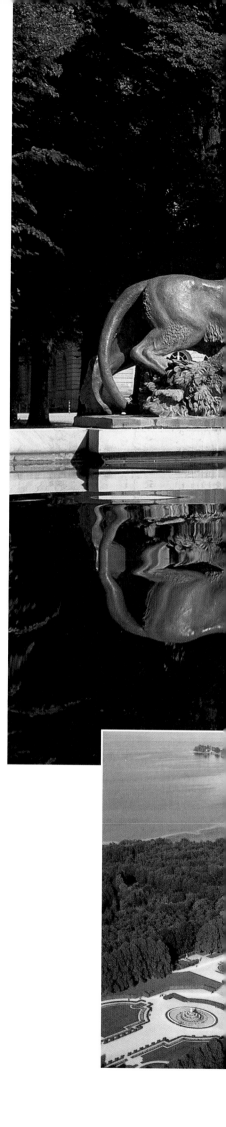

To visit the third of the three major royal residences, one must travel some distance along the foothills of the Alps until Lake Chiem is reached, situated between Munich and Salzburg. Linderhof had not yet been completed when, on May 21, 1879, the cornerstone for the palace at Herrenchiemsee was laid. The plans formed part of a decades-old "Meicost Ettal" project originally intended to be built in the Graswang valley. It pained the king exceedingly that, due to the size of the complex planned, construction at the original site was impossible. After all, the prototype for Ludwig's palace was Versailles. Everything that is opulent and extravagant at Linderhof would be magnified several times at Herrenchiemsee with an incomparable investment of labor and financial means.

Anyone who takes the boat across the lake from Prien to the island Herrenchiemsee will be enthralled by the beautiful landscape and the vast alpine panorama. Maybe the visitor will also wonder about how unusual it is to find a royal palace on a remote island. But if one considers Neuschwanstein, built on a high rocky outcrop, or Linderhof, hidden away in a mountain valley, or the royal retreat at Schachen, way up above the tree line, this location on an island—accessible only by boat—hardly comes as a surprise. King Ludwig sought solitude and found it here like almost nowhere else. It is also certain that for Ludwig, another attraction of the island was its over one-thousand-year-old monastic tradition until the secularization of Bavarian monasteries in 1803. In a certain sense, Ludwig's shrine to the memory of the king of kings, Louis XIV of France, was built on holy ground.

After 1803, the island was bought and re-sold several times until Ludwig acquired it in September 1873. During his second trip to France the following year, he made a thorough tour of Versailles. The planning and building of his new palace progressed at an astounding speed. As of 1881 the king was able to visit his magnificent new residence.

The rooms can be divided into two groups. The "Grands Appartements," dedicated to Louis XIV, take up the south and west wings, while the "Small Appartements," intended for Ludwig II's personal use, are located in the north wing. As at Versailles, the main entrance is not in the middle of the building but

Romantic paths lead through the forest surrounding Herrenchiemsee.

top right: The palace, modelled on Versailles, was intended to be "a pantheon where I shall celebrate the memory of King Louis XIV." (Ludwig II)

bottom: The island Herrenchiemsee lies in close proximity to Frauenchiemsee.

in a side wing. In this way the visitor passes from room to room towards the center of the building before arriving at the triumphant climax of the enfilade in the Chambre de Parade (Grand Bedroom) or the Galerie des Glaces (Hall of Mirrors) beyond. In a subtle way so typical of Ludwig, the journey through the palace affords us an allegorical introduction to the king's view of the world. The allusions are often so unobtrusive as to be hardly noticeable, for example in the stairway.

The visitor can only assume that the contrast of colors here is symbolic—the blue-grey and dark tones of the lower area as opposed to the light, reddish colors above—by comparing this to the prominently-placed figures in the middle of the stairway wall. Diana, the night goddess with the crescent moon in her hair, is shown below, at a spring. She looks down at a nymph and at the water flowing out of a fountain. In a niche above her, the sun god Apollo turns to gaze

43

towards the sun. With his lyre he represents the realm of the arts. If Diana is a reference to Ludwig II, Apollo stands for the Sun King Louis XIV. Not only on account of his disposition, but also due to his activities during different times of the day and night, Ludwig identified himself as a "night king" and, in fact, rose only in the late afternoon and went to bed at dawn. It is a known fact that the French monarch rose with the rising sun, and in so doing supported his own allegory of himself. Like the day and the night, the two kings complement each other in this symbiosis like a mystical, indeed cosmic pair of siblings, at least in the poetic vision of the Bavarian king.

After the Salles des Gardes, where the military victories of the French king are celebrated, and the Première Antichambre du Roi follows the festive, elegant second antechamber, known as the Salon de l'Oeil de Bœuf for the oval window in the cornice. The majestic splendor of this, the largest room in the

following double page:

left: The splendid south stairway is a reconstruction in the style of the 19th century of the 'Escalier des Embassadeurs' in Versailles, which has since been demolished.

right: The room which is known as the 'Salon de l'Oeil de Boeuf' due to its oval windows, is based on the 'Dauphin's Baptism Room' in Versailles.

below: Originally, the master plan by Carl von Effner included a parterre in front of the castle several times larger than can be seen today. The canal on the central axis flows directly into Lake Chiem.

opposite page: Based on the statues at Versailles, mythological female sculptures in lead are arranged along the edge of the water basins.

below: An equestrian statue in the 'Salon de l'Oeil de Boeuf' depicts Louis XIV.

right: Ludwig II never used the 'Chambre de Parade,' as it was meant as a memorial to Louis XIV.

palace, which is dominated by an equestrian statue of Louis XIV, can be explained by the function of its prototype at Versailles. There it was the "Dauphin's Baptism Room." And it was through his baptism that the Bavarian king felt related to the Bourbons. As a reminder: Louis XVI, a grandson of the Sun King, was the godfather of Ludwig's grandfather, Ludwig I, who was born in Strasburg. Ludwig I in turn became the godfather of Ludwig II, because the younger king was born on his nameday. The king had this sacramental link translated in the ceiling painting, lending it the timelessness of antique mythology. We see Aurora, the goddess of the dawn—representing Louis XIV—who gives her spouse Astraeus—who represents the night and therefore also the Bavarian King—a good-morning kiss. At this moment the immense starry nightime sky is brushed side before the daytime sky. Here the theme seen in the stairwell is repeated —only with other figures and means.

The Chambre de Parade which follows is much larger than its counterpart at Versailles. It was presented to the king in 1881 as the first completed room, only three years after the cornerstone of the palace had been laid. It is the heart of the building, a cult room for Louis XIV filled with reddish light from the silk curtains and the careful arrangement of light sources. Everyone who enters here has the immediate im pression that this room was not conceived of as a place for sleeping. Like a monument, the bed stands on a platform under a baldachin and is separated from the rest of the room by a balustrade. The mighty candalabras emphasize the altar-like impression. Continuing the theme from the previous room where dawn is represented, Apollo here rushes before the rising sun across the firmament—a deification of the French sun king whose features he bears.

In the Salle de Conseil (Counsel Hall) beyond, Louis XIV appears on an altar-like painting, also flanked by two candelabras according to the king's specific wish. From the heavenly realm, into which the French king was transported in the preceding room, the divine messenger Mercury brings help and advice to posterity, and thus also to our Ludwig. This is the theme of the ceiling painting.

Flanked by the Salle de la Paix (Hall of Peace) and the Salle de la Guerre (Hall of War) with their mighty medallion reliefs, the Galerie des Glaces extends along the west side of the palace. Almost three hundred feet in length, it is some twenty-five feet longer than the Galerie des Glaces in Versailles. As such, Ludwig meant to give special expression to his admiration for his role model. Except for some structural changes made necessary by the enlarged architecture, it closely imitates its prototype. As at Versailles, the ceiling paintings depict Louis XIV's achievements, reflecting the history of France.

Ludwig visited the castle every year in October. His short stay there resembled a pilgrimage to the temple of the god-like French king. "Sacrosanct" was the word Ludwig used to describe his role model, whose name in French corresponded to his own name in German, and sacrosanct was how he felt himself. Their holy relationship sealed by baptism, a bond which Ludwig considered far superior to "purely physical" lineage, legitimated his own fantasies of

purity and grandeur into which he fled from the unbearable tensions in his soul. In his search for self-assurance, he created a cult around Louis XIV which was clearly a type of worship.

Ludwig II was a night person. In the dark hours, when most people were asleep and dreaming, he wandered through the dreamworld he had created for himself. Ludwig lingered in the Hall of Mirrors only at night and completely alone. It is difficult to imagine the entrancing atmosphere created by two thousand candles burning in forty-four candelabras and thirty-three chandeliers. In the real rooms he "beheld" an unreal vision. The entire palace at Herrenchiemsee was thus conceived of to be looked at, but hardly to be lived in.

Only once, when the king spent a week at the palace in 1885, did he occupy the "Small Appartements" for a slightly longer period. These are adjacent to the splendid rooms in the north wing just described. They also differ from them in many respects. The rooms are considerably smaller. The architectural style is no longer the high Baroque of Louis XIV, but rather the more delicate Rococo form of his successor Louis XVI. And there is no prototype of this at Versailles, which is only logical, since these rooms are not dedicated to the Sun King.

Having become familiar with the palace's symbolism, the visitor immediately recognizes from the blue night lamp in the bedroom that one enters next

that these are the rooms of the "night king." The theme of the embroidered image on the rear panel of the baldachin over the bed also has to do with Ludwig's emotional (and erotic) disposition: the "Triumph of Louis XIV over Vice."

Passing through the study, the Blue Drawing Room is reached, also known as the First Cabinet of Mirrors. Here the play with mirrored images goes so far beyond that of all 18th century precursors: it is only right to see this room as the symbol of Ludwig's distorted relationship with the real world around him. What is actually real, and what is fiction?

The dining room is famous for its "Wishing Table," which can be made to disappear through a trap door in the floor. The king could take his meals here without being disturbed by his servants. But he was never alone. For at the remaining three place settings there were imaginary members of

51

the French court—naturally contemporaries of Louis XIV and XVI, but also
Madame de Pompadour and others. He conversed with them and drank toasts
in their honor.

Through the precious porcelain cabinet, where painted porcelain tiles
are mounted in the walls, doors, and even the writing desk, and the elegant
Small Hall of Mirrors, the north stairwell is reached: a contrast which comes
like a slap in the face. It is nothing more than a rough brick structure devoid of
all decoration. Lack of money made it impossible for the king to complete it.

With a length of almost 300 feet, the Hall of
Mirrors in Herrenchiemsee is some 25 feet
longer than its model in Versailles. It has been
painted with the great deeds of Louis XIV.

Today, many rooms in the palace which are not open to the public are in a similar state. The interior of the north wing, which was torn down after the king's death, was also only a rough brick shell. Wasn't there any money for this either? This was definetely the case for the stairs, but probably not for the other rooms, simply because there were few instructions as to how these rooms were to be furnished. And what could have been put in them! The palace was almost totally un-lived-in, and Ludwig's own needs were fulfilled in the "Grands and Small Appartements." Almost all finished rooms were created only to be seen, and the

53

opposite page: In contrast to the reddish tone of the bedroom dedicated to the Sun King, the bedroom of Ludwig II, the 'night king,' is kept in blue.

right: A Meissen porcelain chandelier with 108 candles as well as 16 sconces illuminated the dining room when the king had dinner at night.

The 'Wishing Table' could be lowered to the floor below through a trap door, so that the shy king could be served without anyone having to enter the room.

same is true of the castle itself with its expansive exterior facades. A look at the ground plan makes it clear that Ludwig by no means intended to copy Versailles. For him it was enough to borrow a few elements which, added together, evoke the prototype but do not reproduce it.

In 1987 a Ludwig II Museum was opened in several of the unfinished rooms on the ground floor. Looking at the documents and photos, and especially such historical objects as the christening gown or the coronation robe, the visitor can gain a deeper understanding of the "last true king," as the French poet Paul Verlaine called Ludwig.

The Altes Schloss (Old Castle) near the steamboat landing stage is well worth a visit. Here Ludwig had several simple rooms furnished from where he could watch the progress being made on the building of his new palace. It was

opposite page, top: The porcelain cabinet is the most intimate room in the palace. Its name derives from the fitments made of porcelain and the porcelain tiles mounted in the doors and the writing desk.

opposite page, bottom: A painting on porcelain representing the allegory of rhetoric serves as a door panel.

right: In contrast to the southern stairway, the one in the north wing—as many other rooms—had to remain unfinished due to a lack of money.

below: On the northern part of the island lies the Old Castle, a former Augustian canon convent. In the room on the top floor of the left wing, the prime ministers of the German states deliberated on the fundamental constitutional law in 1948.

below, right: A mural shows the monastic complex in its Baroque form with the island cathedral, which survives only as a fragment, and a symmetrical garden.

also in these rooms that the prime ministers of the different German states gathered to debate the fundamental constitutional law of the Federal Republic of Germany. To commemorate this historic meeting, a small museum has been opened. Originally the Old Castle was a monastic building of the Baroque period. A mural shows its appearance since the 17th century. The island cathedral nestles against the monastery quadrangle; in front of it there used to be a symmetrically laid out Baroque garden. The complex is surrounded by farm buildings and arable land. Because of numer-ous reconstructions made necessary by the changing use of the building, only a few

Despite the low ceiling of the Emperor's Hall in the Old Castle, the subtle *trompe l'oeil* architecture is very effective. The representations in the vault of mirrors all make reference to food.

opposite page, top: It was a sensation when, in 1960, next to the known Romanesque murals, which a Salzburg master had created in 1130–50, additional representations, such as the head of a prophet (Isaia?), were discovered in an inaccessible place behind the spandrels.

opposite page, bottom: Frauenchiemsee is much smaller than the neighboring island of Herrenchiemsee, but because of a 1,200-year-old convent, its cultural significance is in no way inferior.

The Gothic nave of the convent church on Frauenchiemsee was furnished with Baroque altars in 1688–1702.

parts of the monastery—and still fewer of the island cathedral—are preserved in their original condition. The high Baroque Emperor's Hall on the "prince's floor" has remained unaltered. In 1713–15 the Munich fresco painter Benedikt Albrecht decorated it with portraits of emperors and scenes from the New Testament framed by *trompe l'oeil* architectural scenes. The frescoes and stucco work in the library date from the early Rococo period (around 1738/39) and are attributed to the well-known Munich court painter Johann Baptist Zimmermann and his assistants.

THE FRAUENCHIEMSEE CONVENT

In contrast to Herrenchiemsee, the neighboring island Frauenchiemsee has preserved its character as a convent island. According to ancient sources the convent was founded in 766 by Duke Tassilo III who founded the monks' abbey Herrenchiemsee at the same time. With the exception of a brief interruption after secularization, the convent has been in continuous use right up to the present day. In 1901 it was raised to the status of an abbey by the pope. The convent area can be entered through the porch which was built by King Ludwig the German in 816. Similar to other porches of the same period, there is a chapel in the room over the gateway dedicated to the archangel Michael. The convent church Mariä Opferung (Maria's Sacrifice) still stands on Carolingian foundations from the 9th century. With its portal and frescoes from the Romanesque period, the late Gothic Lierne ribbed vault, and the Baroque altar, the church's architecture reflects the developments of over half a millennium.

THE EXTER HOUSE IN ÜBERSEE

Ludwig II was not the first to discover the charms of the countryside around Lake Chiem. At a time when young painters in France and England were escaping to the country in order to gain new artistic experience outside the dusty walls of the academies, Munich artists were also leaving the city and heading for

the Chiemgau area. As early as 1828 the first painters settled on the Fraueninsel (Ladies' Island), a revolutionary step at that time. For the first time, "nature in all its purity" and the simple life of the rural population would become a subject worthy of art. While artists discovered originality and authenticity—something they had felt lacking in the large, bourgeois city—they also found a new freedom of artistic expression.

Julius Exter (1863–1939) occupies a special position among these painters. A co-founder of the Munich Secession, Exter bought the centuries-old farmhouse "Zum Stricker" in Übersee, a rural community south of Lake Chiem, in 1898. After studying at the Munich Academy he devoted his attention to Impressionism, then later to Symbolism. By today's tastes, his small, expressive landscape paintings of the Chiemgau are the most appealing. With a pigment-laden brush he created veritable fireworks of color and form. He surrounded his house with an idyllic cottage garden which he often made the subject of his paintings, in a similar way to Emil Nolde, to whom he can be compared only for his glowing color schemes. Anyone who lingers a while in the garden during blossom time in spring will understand how Exter had found his Arcadia on earth here. In 1973 his atelier house was bequeathed to the Administration of Castles, Parks and Lakes in Bavaria along with his entire artistic legacy. Since then it has been open to the public.

Julius Exter, *Sunny Morning*, oil painting c. 1925, showing a view across the countryside around Lake Chiem to the Hohenstaufen and Zwiesel mountains.

left: At the farmhouse "Zum Stricker" the painter Julius Exter set up home and a studio for painting.

Julius Exter, *Path of Flowers*, oil painting c. 1920–25, a view of the sea of flowers in the garden around the farmhouse.

Our journey from west to east through the lower alpine region of Bavaria comes to its conclusion at the Königssee (King's Lake). "Painter's Corner" in fact is the name of a spot on the north shore of this alpine lake which inspired the well-traveled naturalist von Humboldt to say, "I consider the Berchtesgaden area, after Naples and Constantinople, to be the most beautiful on earth." Early in the 18th century the lake was already the goal of painters from Vienna and Berlin, Heidelberg and Munich. From "Painter's Corner" we have a good view over the vast expanse of water surrounded by dramatically soaring cliffs, as far as St. Bartholomä church (St. Bartholomew), only reachable by ship, and the hunting lodge of the Wittelsbacher family next to it. Naming all the painters who have painted this and other views around the lake would be a task equal to compiling an encyclopedia of artists. Only a few outstanding personalities should be mentioned here, among them the Berlin classicist architect Karl Friedrich Schinkel who, with paintings and drawings, discovered the area for the landscape painting of the German Romantic period in 1811. Josef Anton Koch was impressed by this circle of mountains as was

St. Bartholomä and the adjacent hunting lodge of the Berchtesgaden provosts shines in the clear spring light of the morning sun.

Ferdinand Olivier, who published a much sought-after series of lithographic views in 1829. All these artists interpreted the beauty and nobility of the nature they found as the expression of the creative power of God. For Caspar David Friedrich, the Watzmann, towering more than eight thousand feet over the lake, became a symbol of the eternity of the Lord. Fifty years later Adolf Menzel spent two summer holidays in Berchtesgaden, the residence of a prince-provost founded in the early 12th century which existed until 1803. This was the starting point for the development of the Königssee region.

In particular one small peninsula in the lower third of the lake attracted the interest of the provosts. It had been formed by the scree washed there by the waters of the Eisbach which has its source below the Watzmann. In 1134 a small Romanesque church dedicated to St. Bartholomä was consecrated on this spot. At the end of the 17th century the strikingly beautiful pilgrimage church was constructed which can still be admired today. The three apses of the choir with their round domes rise over a ground plan in the shape of a clover leaf. The beautiful stucco ornaments and the restrained forms of the altar, chancel, and oratory give the interior its cheerful, rustic appearance.

Immediately following the completion of the church, construction of the hunting lodge next to it was begun. It served the provosts and canons of Berchtesgaden as a summer retreat, whereby hunting played a special role. Until 1715, bears still roamed this isolated mountain region. Naturally fishing was also important.

Following the relegation of the monastery at Berchtesgaden in the aftermath of the secularization, and after its annexation in 1810 to Bavaria,

St. Bartholomä experienced a renewal. The Bavarian kings made the religious establishment their summer residence—and their ancestors still live there during the summer months. St. Bartholomä became one of their favorite places to stay, with Maximilian I, Ludwig I, and Maximilian II organizing large deer and chamois hunts here. Ludwig II, however, had no interest in hunting but felt deeply attached to his area. When at one time the church was in danger of being torn down because of its derelict state, he financed the restoration work from his private funds. The enormously popular prince regent Luitpold was a legendary hunter who, after the deposition of Ludwig II and his mysterious death in Lake Starnberg, tended to the business of ruling over many years with great success.

Today, numerous stories and tales are told of the national solidarity and love of nature shared by the Wittelsbacher rulers, who all—some more often than others—spent time at St. Bartholomä. Since then the small but unusually appealing church standing before its majestic mountain backdrop has impressed itself in the consciousness of countless visitors as the symbol of the Upper Bavarian cultural landscape.

Front cover: Neuschwanstein, view of upper court
Front flap: Ferdinand von Piloty, Ludwig II in a general's uniform and coronation vestments, 1865 (Ludwig II Museum at Herrenchiemsee)
Back flap: The Hall of Mirrors, Herrenchiemsee

Photographic credits: all pictures are from the archives held at the Bavarian Administration of State Castles, Palaces, Gardens, and Lakes with the exception of pp. 1, 3 bottom, 11 top left, 14 top, 24 bottom, 38 center: Matthias Michel, mm vision, Erling; pp. 3 center, 13, 23, 27 top, 30, 31, 35 bottom, 49, 54, 55: Neumeister Fotografie, Munich; S. 39, 59 bottom, 63: Thomas Peter Widmann, Regensburg; p. 12: Gerold Jung, Ottobrunn; p. 38 bottom: Norbert Dinkel, Munich

Cartography: Anneli Nau, Munich

5th revised edition, 2010
© Prestel Verlag, Munich · Berlin · London · New York, 2000

The Library of Congress Cataloguing-in-Publication data is available;
British Library Cataloguing-in-Publication Data: a catalogue record for this book is available from the British Library; Deutsche Bibliothek holds a record of this publication in the Deutsche Nationalbibliografie; detailed bibliographical data can be found under: http://dnb.ddb.de

Prestel, a member of Verlagsgruppe Random House GmbH
Prestel Verlag, Königinstraße 9, 80539 Munich
Tel. (089) 242908-300, fax (089) 242908-335;
www.prestel.de
4 Bloomsbury Place, London WC1A 2QA
Tel. (020) 7323 5004, fax (020) 7636 8004;
900 Broadway, Suite 603, New York, NY 10003
Tel. (212) 995-2720, fax (212) 995-2733
www.prestel.com

Translated from the German by Jacqueline Guigui-Stolberg
Edited by Christopher Wynne
Designed and typeset by Norbert Dinkel, Munich
Lithography by ReproLine, Munich
Printed and bound by TBB Banska Bystrica

Printed in Germany
Printed on acid-free paper

ISBN 978-3-7913-2386-2 (English edition)
ISBN 978-3-7913-2376-3 (German edition)
ISBN 978-3-7913-2470-8 (Italian edition)
ISBN 978-3-7913-2471-5 (French edition)
ISBN 9783-7913-2613-9 (Japanese edition)